Romance In A Modern World

ANTONIO LIRANZO

Other Books By Antonio Liranzo

Falling Angel: Rising Phoenix (2020)

For Updates Follow

Instagram.com/AntonioILiranzo
Twitter.com/AntonioILiranzo
AntonioLiranzo.com

Copyright © 2021 by

First Printing, 2021

Cover Design: Lioputra
Back Cover Design: Richard Bohan
Inside Book Designs: Michelle Riofrio
Editors: Viterbo Liranzo & Audrey Brown

This goes to all the hopeless romantics out there. If you love to love and aren't afraid to show vulnerability, this one's for you.

Acknowledgments

I can't believe this is my second book in less than a year! Thank you to everyone who has supported me and purchased a copy. This has been a wild ride and a beautiful new beginning. I hope this book takes you on a ride of romance you'll never forget!

To my editors and proofreaders: First and foremost, my brother, Viterbo Liranzo. I love that this has been our second book together within a year! I love having you on this journey with me, your grammatical eyes and knowledge always help me more than you'll ever know, Thank you! My second editor, Audrey Brown. Girl, I love you so much! It's amazing to have a beautiful human be part of this journey. Half of these poems, I would vent to you about certain experiences, you understand it and you get me! Thank you so much, love you! Samuel Rider, I asked you last minute to proofread my book and help me make some last minute edits, thank you for helping! You have been there for a lot of these stories/moments, you have helped me get through some tough times with amazing therapeutic conversations and wine nights. Love you!

Shoutout to my artists that worked with me, Lioputra, thank you for the amazing artwork for my cover, you made my romantic fantasy land come to life. My second artist and friend, Richard Bohan, I always love working with you. From my book release for my first book "Falling Angel: Rising Phoenix", to now creating the back cover of my new book. Thank you for being a great friend and creator. My third artist, Michelle Riofrio, the details in your sketches are beautiful! You created some amazing promotional images for me during my first book release, I am so happy to have your work in this book!

2020 has been an insane year! It brought breakups with friends and a partner. But through it all, I was able to find ways to work on myself. I started attending therapy and learning about my sensitive tendencies. I discovered the truth and empathetic tendencies within myself.It's amazing to finally know who I am and what my mission on this earth is. A part of this mission is writing love poems to the universe and sharing them with my readers. Enjoy the ride!

Preface

As a human who wears their heart on their sleeve, I am notorious for experiencing hurt, heart break, and being used. The battle between using my heart and my head has never come easy. I've never listened to my intuition and always found "Love" in the wrong kind of partner. This romantic modern world I created takes you on a ride inside my heart and all the feelings I have. I talk about breakups, threesomes, meaningless sex, meaningful sex, being cheated on, family and friend love, marriage, moving on, lessons learned, and empathy.

I do live in a romantic fantasy land at times, and sometimes, reality hits me in the face and says, "Antonio, get your head out of the clouds!" This book is intended to show you the simultaneous struggle of wanting to be in a relationship but also to not forget that loving yourself and surrounding yourself with people who have good energy around you is just as important.

A message to my readers, give love and spread more love, and please, just be a good fucking person!

Contents

2
IN A

3
MODERN

4
WORLD

ROMANCE IN A MODERN WORLD

1

Romance

Social construction
The art of destruction
Channeling your feels in apps
Is life all but a trap?

A Little Crazy

My love
Like Sweethearts on Valentines Day
Crushes so easily
Beware!

Bloody
Vulnerable
Dangerous
Love.

Hope you can take the pain
My heart strings are sharp like barbed wire
Pull me the wrong way
You might be pricked.

Beware
Be aware
Be warned

For this bite may be fun at first, but cheating leads
to cannibalism with me.

I love to love
It may make me a little crazy
A wounded heart
With fangs that bite back.

Hope you're up for the ride!

Can You Handle Me?

Vulnerability is my playing field
I am not afraid of a wounded heart
I will give it my all
Sometimes too much.

Sacrificial moments
Bleeding out empathy
Are you going to carry this wounded human?
Can you handle me?

I am not going to change
How much I love
I fucking care about people and life
So I will ask you one more time...

Can you handle me?

Mirrors

A mirrored room
A hot summer night
In Coney Island
The sky is like cotton candy.

This vicious cycle feels like a ferris wheel
Round and round
A fake face like a clown
Manic speed like a rollercoaster.

That moment in the mirrored room
Your facial reactions
Reflecting back to yourself
A face so emotionless.

The Good

I got that good good
You got that bad bad
Tongue tied talking
Baby I don't like to lie.

Fall feels like summer
You know that first day of the season
On the ferry to this fun island
Nothing but smiles and cheeky plans.

A weekend with you is timeless
I don't wear a watch because with you, time is bet-
ter left untold
A sunset tells the ending
When I'm with you, my night is always just begin-
ning...

To the memories of the summer, to the dark nights
in the winter
I cherish my time being with your uplifting energy
<3.

Dreams & Fog Machines

Bubbles
Dreams
Fog machines
Tequila shots.

This hazy house party
Trying to find the right one in this messy crowd
What a time to be alive?
With social media and instant gratification.

Sarcasm is my best strategy
To show I am attempting to communicate
In a vain world
Can you grab me and we ride along the hills?

Like a scene in *La La Land*

Making out on top of the Hollywood Hills
Silence and your leather jacket
What a time to be alive!

Is there satisfaction?
Or am I just using sarcasm to make me think I like
this moment?
The vanity of the people I meet
Makes me realize that the bubbles, dreams and fog
machines are just an illusion.

... To cover the insecurities that you have.

Watermelon Blow Pop

That sweet taste with the first lick
I like that excited look in your eyes
I am intrigued
I want to taste more.

The high atmosphere with you
Bright lights, city adventures
Watermelon is my favorite flavor
Besides you!

Moments of crashing and colliding
Biting down on the last bit of my lollipop
Chewing the saturated watermelon gum
This sweet feeling at night will last with you for-
ever.

Your Mistake

5 AM booty call
A troll
A boy who is lost in the candy store
I'm sorry for your misguided judgement.

Can't get over your mistake
This phoenix doesn't wait
Oh, you want to re-explain yourself?
You did it through text, yet again, timely excuses.

Seeing me out at night
Someone else's arm around me
Anger rises, eyes widen, fists clenched
Decide...

You want me now?
I guess taking six months
Gets me bored...

Have fun watching!

Realize your mistakes get in the way of your happi-
ness ...

Sex & Lives

Boots and thighs
I will play with your lies
Zip and shut
You in my mouth.

Lips and thirst
I am so parched
Celibacy is overrated
Take me home!

New York City and nightlife
Ripped jeans and temptation
Tension and release
I guess it's just me tonight...

Is This Real Life?

Infatuation
I'm a dreamer
Embodiment
I'm a giver.

Art
Can I be your canvas?
The touch of your brush
I never loved goosebumps till now.

Is this real life?
Denial is a primary color of mine
The light for me is always short lived
Is this the end of the love tunnel?

Fantasies
I live in an idealist world
Romance in a Modern World?

No. This is a realistic world.

My hope is strong
My faith in the one
No knight in shining armor
I want mutual respect and a visionary.

Understand my devotion
Live in my dreamland
Respect my ambition
Be the Bonnie to my Clyde.

I think I may have found someone...

Try Ways To Three Ways

I'm not from this town
You see me on the prowl
Grabbing your mans hand
Walking my way.

You say "Hey, We saw you last night"
I say "Too bad we didn't hang last night"
One drink leads into 3 drinks
Which leads to us 3 walking to the bathroom.

I usually want attention from 1
But something about you 2 makes me want more
The look on your face when you see your
boyfriend having fun
Who knew this New Yorker in wonderland would
be wandering your land.

My Family Is My Rock

I was down and out
My brother hearing my voice broken
I always have the worst luck
My mom knows way too well about these men.

Going home, sad and heart broken
My friends are here to help me with mimosas
Oh, how I love girl brunches
These ladies are my hype women.

Wine nights with my besties
Encouraging me to move on
Self reminder that I am that bitch!
You never let a guy get you down.

My mom is my inspiration of taking no crap from a man!

My brother is my solid rock that is always a listening ear.

My friends, you all get me through every day.

The encouragement, love, gratitude and of course wine!!

This is family <3.

Apps

Pretending to be someone
A poker face is ready to be put on
Are you a big shark in this game?
Or, just a catfish?

This Modern World we are in
People swipe, people like, people lie
I want this, no, I WANT THAT
Who knew this era of romance would have so many
choices.

Cyber sex
More like edited sex
Plenty of fish in the sea
Well I'm a vegetarian.

I'd rather dive in a garden of fresh vegetables
Have organic interactions and moments

Know the energy in my body is fully vital
Fruition is my nutrition to my intuition of know-
ing...

There is more love outside than in the virtual
world.

2

In A

No one satisfies my needs
I am on a journey of freedom and self love
I have the right to be picky with who I let in
Working so hard to be where I am
A true leader will never let the weak win.

I LOVE YOU

Yes
I said
The
L Word.

You know
I am a sucker
For
Corny moments.

I wanted to say it on a special day
But when you know
You know
And I know that, I love you!

Now that I said it
We can soak in it
Enjoy that our love is out there

I love that I finally said I love you!

Society teaches us
To be weary when saying these three words
But fuck it
I LOVE YOU!

My Forever

I always wanted this moment
I am a big lover
Sometimes too much for my own good
The way you value me lets me know this is okay!

I have so much baggage, I may be damaged
Thank you for understanding
Thank you for guiding
Thank you for loving me.

Holding your hand down the aisle
The crowd full of our family and friends smiling
There were so many moments in my life, where I
thought this wasn't possible
Can someone honestly love me this much besides
my mom and brother?

You have become my safety net

We have built an empire together
Thanks for taking the chance on me
Thanks for showing me that I can love and be
loved.

Romance is a journey
This Modern World is crazy
I've always lived in wonderland
Thanks for bringing me to my forever land.

Playing The Game

I thought I liked you
Three months later
Have my feelings changed?
Looking at you does not give me the same satisfac-
tion, I received three months ago.

I don't know how to say this
I'm usually the one getting cut off after four weeks
It's usually my love karma
The roles have been reversed!

I hate being on your end
I don't know if I can tell you
It's over.
Have I become a bad person?
Why am I overthinking this?

How can my feelings change?

I was never a fuck boy.
Do I know the truth?
Knowing takes time.

I am so sorry
I have to let you know this isn't working anymore
No excuses.
But I need time to myself.

Dangerous Love

White v-neck
Black jacket
Skinny jeans
Chelsea shoes.

Eye contact
Let me buy you a drink
Next thing I know
Hands on my hips, my lips on his.

The clock strikes at midnight
I'm no cinderella
Wicked is more in my DNA
After midnight is always more fun.

(B)ad (B)oy (E)nergy
Yours captivates me
I'm in wonderland.

Will you come with me, down the rabbit hole?

Chasing

To chase
To choose
To be chosen ...

Reaching out is great
No reciprocation is substantial
Meeting me halfway is respectful
No effort is miserable.

There's that turning point
Where enough is enough
I've had my fair share
Of tug and war.

The difference is, I'm not in fifth grade anymore
You like to play with strings
Maybe learn guitar
Because this heart is the chosen one.

The Sun Is Rising

My love for you is on a horizon
The sun is rising
The joy I get from that smile
Is like snow on Christmas.

I hate the thought of you with someone else
I can't tame you
I can't blame you
But during this moment you're mine.

Like fine red wine
Your taste is enticing
Never a hangover with you
Thanks for being the bottle, holding my heart!

Pink Lips & A Cigarette

Entering a beam filled room.
Strobe lights.
Flashing.
I can only make sense of your shadow
Cheek bones, pink lips and a cigarette.

Grabbing my hand.
It's so dark.
Do I follow you into tonight's dark mystery jour-
ney?
Hands on my waist.
Following the leader.

11:11 make a wish
So high on this energy
The genie heard me.

My 11:11 wish is here.

Bad behavior.
Naughty nature.
Fire chemistry.
Be my mister?

To this twister of wishes and non regretful nights.

A Weekend Moment

Momentary emotions
Running high
A hand on my hip
Tingles all over my body.

You are my security blanket
For the time being...
Are these feelings real?
Or is it the timing?

Time is a made up thing
This moment is made of moments
Is there going to be a moment post high?
Will this fizzle out?!

We say goodbye

Hoping for a hangout again
I wake up the next day
Remembering that fun moment.

Life is full of different moments
This was a weekend thing
I am ready for my next moment
With or without you.

Prism

My heart is shiny
Like a diamond
Wait
Are you the diamond in the rough?

Please be gentle
I have a tough exterior
But inside
Fragile!

It's mirroring triggers
So emotionally unstable
Overstimulated
It feels too alive!

This precious organ
Takes on white aura
Transforming it to various colors

If you handle it with kindness and respect, it will guide you to a more colorful life.

Let's Getaway

I just want to be with you forever
Running away from our problems
Can we act a little immature
For once?

Running on the sand
Waves are crashing
I am wearing your flannel
It's October, but you make it feel like it's July.

We have all week together
Where are we going next?
We have no set plans
Just us and the world tonight.

Holding hands
Skipping down the wine aisle
What should we drink tonight?

I can't wait to cuddle and watch a movie.

Life isn't perfect
But can I have this moment forever?
I feel so alive right now
I want to get away from reality.

In this moment
You are my reality
You're my now
This moment is ours!

When we end this week
Let's dream about this moment
I want to be your ride or die
We are chasing the sun and we have no plan to
stop.

Euphoric

Bright lights
Strobe lights
That reflection
I find in your eyes

I'm rolling with molly
Sweating
Embracing the euphoric energy
Be my lolli?

Danger?
I'm intrigued
You're worried you may misguide me?
Oh, hunni, I'm the sweetest devil you'll ever meet.

Feeling the energy around me
I'm fatally in love with the high of life
Auras shining so bright

There is no current hate in my life.

This feels like a mystical forest
I'm lost but not alone
I'm dancing with this room
Am I looking for another soul?

I am the enigma of me
I am the proof of what I need
To always remember
That either with you or alone.

I am always my own euphoria!

Thinking Of You

What are we?
Sitting at home, waiting for a text
This addiction
Of the chase.

I thought games were for toddlers
Waiting for you
I feel like
A little boy being pushed on the playground by his crush.

Feeling stuck on the couch
Rereading our messages is my snack preference
Your replies are my daily programs
But is this journey the TV guide to my heart?

Romantico

Roses are red
Violets are blue
My mouth is better
On you!

Dreamy
Spiritual dates
Inner connection
You have caught my attention.

These American guys can't touch you
This inner bliss
Will make me miss
The true meaning of romance.

Sei simpatico
Mi sono persi
I'm a lover who is a hopeless romantic

Meeting you reminded me that romance isn't hope-less!

Sei Romantico.

Me Time

Space
Comfort
Relax
Inner thoughts.

Scary ideas
All alone, is it time to think?
Nervous to do nothing
Is this how it is to do nothing?

Realizing my freedom
Being alone isn't so bad
Being your own friend
Is step one to happiness.

Why was I afraid to be alone?
Thoughts are scary
Is it weird I'm comfortable doing nothing?

Introverted...

Me time!

Drinks

Drunk
Trying to work this out
Hard to hear you
Do you mean what you say?

You're stumbling
Are you sure?
That you mean what you say?
Drunk mumble.

They say true feelings are said when drunk
Well if that's true
Then I might as well have been a psychic
Because your truth is traumatizing.

Cold

Twiddling my thumbs
An involuntary plunge
I am sinking twenty feet deep
Lost in the arctic, that is your heart .

Winter time is my favorite
Feeling cold in the snow
Makes me feel alive
Like a snowman, there's no fire in your eyes.

3

Modern

Never thought I would be so wounded
My love infection is too real
I want desperately to be loved
Yet, I am in love with someone transparent.

A Snack

Gum
Pop
Pants
Drop.

I use these words as a metaphor
For the emotions I feel
Like a seagull with a bag of chips
I'm that snack you want with a dip.

Sun rays to stingrays
I don't mind being stung
Rosy cheeks with a splash of rosé
Your vibes got me wine drunk.

Feelings so high
Who needs a line?!
I'm beaming and glowing

This chemistry is flowing.

Sometimes I think dark
Can your love be my spark?
My vision is narrow
Can you light my tunnel?

Sex

You see it as a transaction
I take it as an interaction
You're so alone, it's your safety zone
I'm so comfortable, it's made my connection grow.

If sex had monetary value
You would be an investor
I would be a broke artist
Choosing quality over quantity.

Trying to find love?
More like, trying to find lust
Trying to find the one?
More like, trying to be in one.

I'm here for love with some spice
I don't want to live with empty lust
Lust can be fun in the moment

But moments are only temporary.

Aloneness can be forever...

Temptation

Red light district
My brown eyes
Locking on your
Jawline.

Lips perched
Body language
Head turns
Staring back at me.

Lonely people in this club
Needing validation
I wonder
Are you feeling alone?

Needing a break from this crazy life
Frustration at an all time high
I wonder

Am I feeling alone?

A glance back
Head nods
He moves toward me
Grips me in!

Is this what not feeling alone feels like?
In a tight grip
I loosen up
The need for validation is tricky.

Full eye contact
A kiss
An ass grab
We leave.

Red light district
His blue eyes
Locking on my jawline
Loneliness connecting with loneliness.

Same Old, Same Old

Excuses!
Excuses!
Excuses!

Uses tissues for their excuses!
Uses words for their excuses!
Uses persuasion for their excuses!

Sounds like a broken record
A symphony I don't care for
Bored from the crack in that voice
That same old broken record.

Same old lies!
Same old drama!
Same old excuses!

Finally decided to throw out that record
I'd rather stream my options
Records can scratch and wear out
Seems like you both have that in common.

Same old, Same old excuses!

Growing

I miss the warmth of your body
Why did you decide to do this?
I can't sleep with all these thoughts
Is it something I could have done better?

I believe I give true love
It's sufficient enough for your love
Maybe it wasn't me and it was you
When something happens, why do we self doubt?

I want to grow!
I refuse to be hurt!

4

World

Being free is the key to life...
The problem is that my door is stuck!

Free To Be & Free To Love

The limit doesn't exist
I give into my creative expression
I'm an enigma
My heart is all I trust.

I am happy where I am
Maybe being trapped isn't so bad after all
The bliss has always been within.

Trust your gut, it will spare your sentence
Your actions are your friends
How you feel is how you feel
You won't regret it.

Until that person breaks through my door.
I am here living in solo nirvana.

A soul has too much power
I am free, I am me, I am the lock to my key!

Right Timing

It wasn't the right timing
Thought I was your "Mr. Right"
But you weren't ready for commitment
Every road comes to an end.

It's how you pick yourself up after a missed route
Is your GPS guiding your journey?
Your signal may not be detected
I may not be the service that you are trying to
find...

F*** Boy Fun

I wanted a transition
You wanted an intermission
I was your mister
You preferred guys playing tongue twister.

I am leveling up
I'm taking the elevator to the penthouse without
you
How's the stairs to floor two?
Is hitting a plateau fun?

I'm on a self love grind
You're on a self sabotage high
I'm on that money grind
You're the meaning of, boy bye!

Who knew being a bad bitch was so fun?
One day you are going to run from

Seeing all the beauty this goddess has become
Makes you think, was it worth that fuck boy fun?

Old School To New School

This theatrical production
Overdosing with your pills and potions
Killing my ambition with your transmission
I didn't know this was an audition!

Obstacles of the course
You belittle me the most
Treason without reason
I am the pen to the signature.

Understanding my meaning
For the king of this season
Delusion and distraction
I'm over this traction.

We are here to love and feel

Yet, inner demons decide
What the truth is
I'm not reaching for a reason.

That you can't see me, because it's not your "season".

Cosmic Love

Rays of light
Cosmic sensation
Stars in the night
You're my temptation.

Venus is calling
Lust for living is real.
If you were the milky way
I would be your sun.

They say space isn't limited
They say the sky has no limit
They say love can defy gravity
I say let me define your love.

Passion

When you touch me
I feel fire
Your mouth
Juicy like a peach.

The way you kiss me
I can't even put in words
It gets me so high
I am orgasmically speechless.

All your tongue
Those soft lips
You kiss me
Like you mean it.

I may sound weird
But, I think kissing
Is better

Than sex.

A human
That can make me melt with their mouth
Is so attractive to me
Our mouths are hugging and never letting go.

This moment
I feel safe
I feel loved
Damn, I feel sexy.

Why don't we
Go lay down
Put on some slow music
Drink red wine.

Licking your lips
Hugging my body
You match it, by
Hugging my lips.
Now, that's what I call passion!

A Soundtrack To Love

We go out
I get the car
You got the dinner
We are vibing.

Those first few months of liking each other
Exploring your body
Licking your lips
Your touch has me on a trip.

Holding hands on date four
My inner saboteur is out to play
Romantic sparks shut him up
Experiences like this, finally have me out of my
head!

No over thinking
Just feeling
Setting the stage for me
To finally feel free.

Society tells us
We should take it slow
But something about this
Feels like a 80's romantic movie.

We stick middle fingers up to critics
Run around New York City in our denim
Playing our favorite soundtrack to love
Because this love is picture perfect.

Why Can't We Be?

I guess our stars didn't align
Like a shooting star
With a blink
You can miss its shine!

Wrong timing?
Or, was it the right?
Just wrong people
Who are living in separate galaxies.

Like comic book rivals
Our philosophies on life clash
Strong opinions
Dimming our light.

One person jokes

The other takes offense
The tables turn
Now you're playing defense.

The spark that brought me life
Is now dimming my soul
Earth revolves around the sun
Why can't we revolve around love?

You will be missed
The shooting star that once was
Is now gone in the dark sky
Maybe we will meet in a different universe <3.

Safe Sex

I miss dating you
But, I also miss
Fucking
You!

Safe sex
I'm not talking about a condom
I'm not talking about PREP
I'm talking about you!

You make me feel safe
As an empath, I trust your energy
I am not into one night stands
I want your body forever.

No STD worries
No feeling depleted
No transactional sex

There was a spiritual connection in the bedroom.

We were good in bed
Your magical touch
Our synchrony was orgasmic
But(t)...

We weren't good at dating
I thought about being friends with benefits with
you
The only benefit would be safe sex and cuddling
Our hearts would be too involved.

The reason you gave me safe sex is because our
hearts were so connected in the past, my soul was
yours to be with forever, now it seems as forever is
never...

We Are Not Meant To Be

Simply
Let's just clear the air
We were not meant to be
It's a harsh reality.

We keep trying to make something work
I truly did love you
Maybe, this was meant to be another kind of rela-
tionship
This is a reality check for both of us!

We are not meant to be...

Life partners, instead let's be another form of soul-
mates.

Lessons

Not everyone is meant to get along
You taught me that
Everyone has different opinions
You taught me that.

People have emotional baggage
You showed me that
Relationships and love scares people
You showed me that.

Fighting is so draining
We felt that
Make up sex and cuddles are amazing
We felt that.

I need to protect my aura
I learned that
I need to work on letting people in

I learned that.

Life is full of lessons
Being romantically involved with you
Was a three month intensive
To the labor of love <3.

The Breakup + Summer Memories

It felt so safe
We felt like a unit
Was this a magnetic attraction?
Or was it a fatal attraction?

A gravitational pull
We were flying so high
But we could only stay up for so long
A crash was destined to happen.

We are descending on different levels
Having flashbacks
Trying to make things work
But it's too late.

Maybe in a different timeline
I do believe in a parallel universe
Let's not rush this karmic timing
What's meant to be is meant to be.

I can always look back
At those memories
The enjoyable moments
I will keep a fresh face in my memory even though
my heart aches.

......

Waking up on the boat
Hungover but excited
I get to see your face
I can't wait to hug your body.

A magical Sunday
Beach, sun and rosè
You look so good in your speedo
Holding my hand all night, let's play!

Bringing you back during the evening
Undressing you
You're mine forever
Penetrating you and your soul.

You were my sweet summer moment

You were the beginning of my fall
Even though gravity pulled us down
I will always be high looking back .

Even though we may not be on the same page,
thank you for the amazing memories!

Always Love Yourself

Life and love have obstacles
It may be challenging
Remember you are worth it!
Don't be afraid to feel!

If love comes around
Be open to it
You deserve it
It may hurt and sting!

In this Modern World
It's hard to date
But love is more than just what we see in the
movies
Love comes in all flavors!

From, family
To friends
The true love
That remains number one, is yourself!

Feel
Love
Let Be
But remember.

It's cool to be kind and give love
Projection of past trauma or fear
Can lead to further unhappiness
Read the room but also READ YOURSELF <3.

Meaningless Sex

My soul
Is worth more
Than
My penis.

That one hour in bed with you
Seems so nice in the moment
I am getting off from you
Releasing my needs.

But when the climax is over
And the moment has gone
We only met each others bodies
Do we even know each other?

Some people feel sexual energy
I am one of those people
I need a safety realm

To release my sensual side.

When I am thinking with my other head
I can easily get distracted
But, as life goes on
My intuition is speaking.

No more body count
This number game is getting old
I always disliked math
Numbers and bodies aren't fulfilling my soul.

I want conversation
Safety
Love
Care.

To get this body
You need to understand my brain
Feel my soul
Know me...

My soul is genuine
I am a diamond in the rough
Trying to wear me like jewelry
Can you find the key...

To my heart necklace?

Dear Future Partner,

Dear Future Partner,
I have been through a lot
I may have wounds and baggage
But I do my best not to project.

I am a huge lover
Sometimes that love spills over
This diamond in my chest
Has the toughest fragility.

I am not saying you have to watch me
I am a grown human
I just want to let you know
I am not perfect and neither are you.

We will fight over stupid things

Let's just remember
That real love and true emotions
Conquer all.

I want someone that is emotionally intelligent
Someone who gets me
Someone who feeds my soul
I want to have a safe realm with you.

Coexisting
Two lives working together
I will have my moments
But we will make it worthwhile!

Reciprocation is big for me
Just know I am highly sensitive
I expect the same respect and love back
Cherish me, because I am about to cherish you so
much.

I vow to be completely honest
I am known for being vulnerable
I've learned to protect my heart when needed
Only bring that good love to me, I don't do toxic
shit.

Dear Future Partner,
You could be my end game
Even if we don't last long

Know that I am the kind of ex that wants to be
your friend and wish you well.

I guess
What I am trying to say, is
I am ready for the next chapter!
I am more conscious of what I want and what I deserve.

Dear Future Partner,
Is that you?

Empathy & Me

This feeling I can't explain
Why do I feel so heavy?
Increased anxiety
This world can be scary.

This word introduced itself to fill my head
Empathy!
Have I found a word
That can help me label everything I have ever felt?

I look back
I cry for my mom
I feel sad for my brother
I cry for the unfortunate.

This superpower
Is a sixth sense
A double edge sword
It's good to feel even if it means to hurt.

Do I hide this side of me?
How do I protect my soul?
I've had a wall built for so long
It sucks to hide.

Playing this hard ass
But in reality
My heart bleeds emotions and
...Tears!

Overwhelming feelings
I sometimes don't know what to do
Overstimulation
Sometimes I can't think.

I try to be a good person
I can get in my own way
Building a self wall
Just dims my light.

Maybe, I'm learning
Maybe, It's ok to take the pain
I can grow from all these emotions
Why hide behind a wall?

I'm tired of hiding
It's time to embrace what the universe has in store
for me
It's time to use my power

As long as I protect my aura, I will be okay!

I just want to love
I want to give light
I want to help heal
Sometimes I lose myself along the way.

Maybe this time I won't
I feel like I can grow on this empathy path
Energy and emotions guide me
Maybe, being an empath isn't so bad.

Empath is spelled; **E M P A T H**
Maybe, if I help **ME** on this **PATH**
I can discover that being an empath
Is a blessing not a curse!

Thank You

To all the lovers, romantics, empaths, and sensitive humans reading this; I want you to know that it's okay to LOVE, it's okay to be vulnerable, it's OKAY TO BE HEARTBROKEN, give your all in everything that you do and love. LOVE HARD and NEVER DIM YOUR LIGHT OR SOUL! I hope this book helps show you that showing LOVE is hard but also rewarding!

About The Author

   Antonio Liranzo is a performer and writer from
New York. He grew up in Long Island and moved to
the city to follow his artistic pursuits. Writing poetry
has been a passion since he was a child and has always
dreamed of having his work published so he may
share his passion with the public. As a mental health
advocate, poetry has also become a source of therapy.
Sharing these life stories in a poetic form with a little
help and inspiration from pop culture, it's Antonio's
mission to share in hopes that his words can be re-
lated to and be just as therapeutic to his readers. Be
sure to check out his previous book, Falling Angel:
Rising Phoenix that was published in 2020. Thank you
for your continuous support. Go out there and love
freely and fiercely!
   Instagram : @AntonioILiranzo
   Twitter: @AntonioILiranzo

CPSIA information can be obtained
at www.ICGtesting.com
Printed in the USA
LVHW012328210221
679514LV00007B/877

9 781087 937113